HYMNS
with a Classical Flair

15 TRADITIONAL FAVORITES ARRANGED BY PHILLIP KEVEREN

— PIANO LEVEL —
INTERMEDIATE

ISBN 978-1-5400-2478-7

Copyright © 2018 by HAL LEONARD LLC
International Copyright Secured All Rights Reserved

Visit Hal Leonard Online at
www.halleonard.com

Visit Phillip at
www.phillipkeveren.com

Contact Us:
Hal Leonard
7777 West Bluemound Road
Milwaukee, WI 53213
Email: info@halleonard.com

In Europe contact:
Hal Leonard Europe Limited
Distribution Centre, Newmarket Road
Bury St Edmunds, Suffolk, IP33 3YB
Email: info@halleonardeurope.com

In Australia contact:
Hal Leonard Australia Pty. Ltd.
4 Lentara Court
Cheltenham, Victoria, 3192 Australia
Email: info@halleonard.com.au

AMAZING GRACE
New Britain

Traditional American Melody
Arranged by Phillip Keveren

BLESSED ASSURANCE

Assurance

Music by PHOEBE PALMER KNAPP
Arranged by Phillip Keveren

Tenderly (♩. = c. 60)

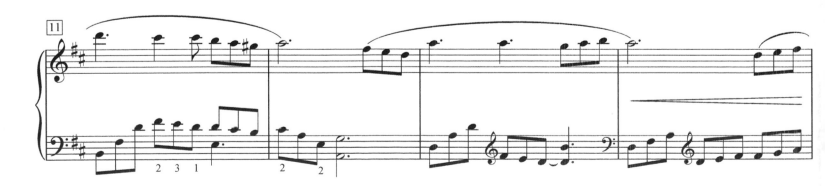

FAITH OF OUR FATHERS

St. Catherine

Music by HENRI F. HEMY
and JAMES G. WALTON
Arranged by Phillip Keveren

Expressively, with rubato (♩. = c. 69)

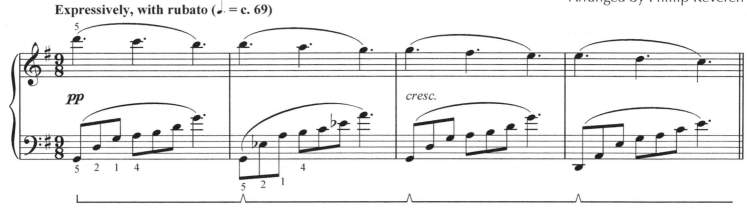

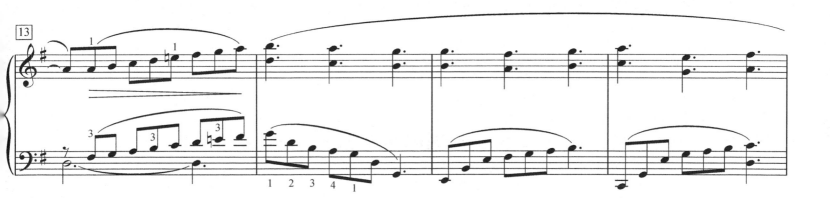

FAIREST LORD JESUS

Crusaders' Hymn

Music from *Schlesische Volkslieder*
Arranged by Phillip Keveren

HIS EYE IS ON THE SPARROW
Sparrow

Music by CHARLES H. GABRIEL
Arranged by Phillip Keveren

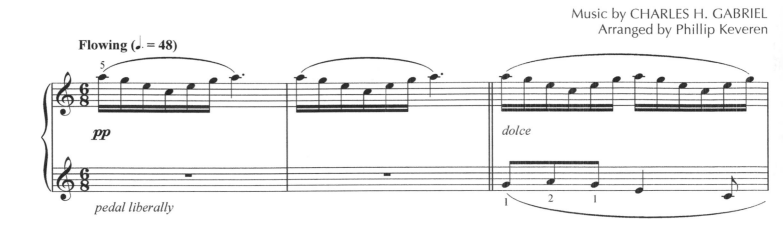

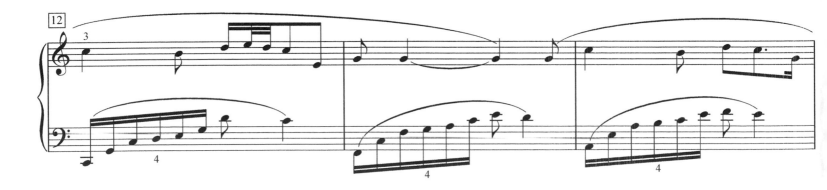

HOW FIRM A FOUNDATION
Foundation

Early American Melody
Arranged by Phillip Keveren

IN THE GARDEN

Garden

Words and Music by
C. AUSTIN MILES
Arranged by Phillip Keveren

Quietly, with freedom ($\textbf{.} = 42$)

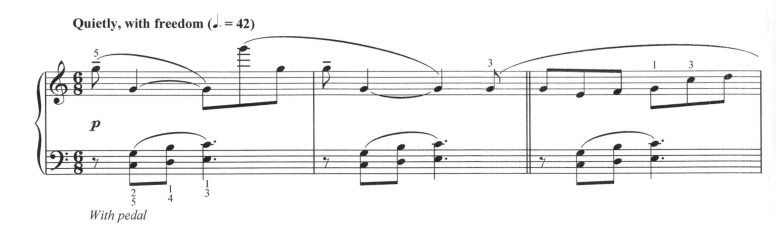

JUST A CLOSER WALK WITH THEE

Closer Walk

Traditional
Arranged by Phillip Keveren

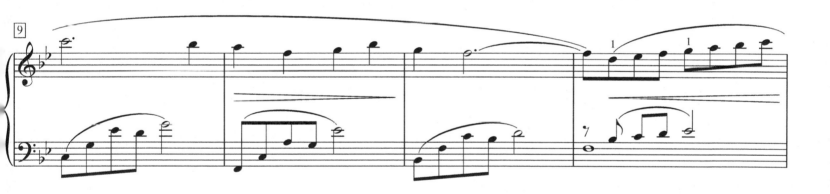

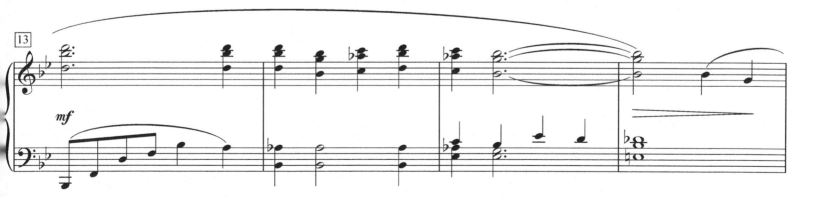

20

NEARER, MY GOD, TO THEE

Bethany

Music by LOWELL MASON
Arranged by Phillip Keveren

THE OLD RUGGED CROSS
Old Rugged Cross

Words and Music by
REV. GEORGE BENNARD
Arranged by Phillip Keveren

ROCK OF AGES
Toplady

Music by THOMAS HASTINGS
Arranged by Phillip Keveren

TAKE MY LIFE AND LET IT BE

Hendon

Music by HENRY A. CÉSAR MALAN
Arranged by Phillip Keveren

With energy (♩ = 120)

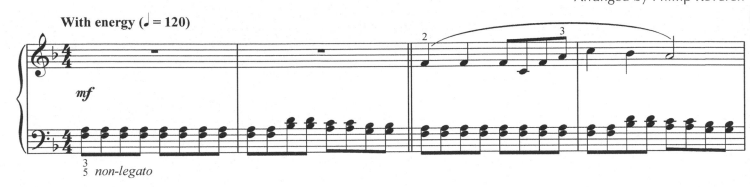

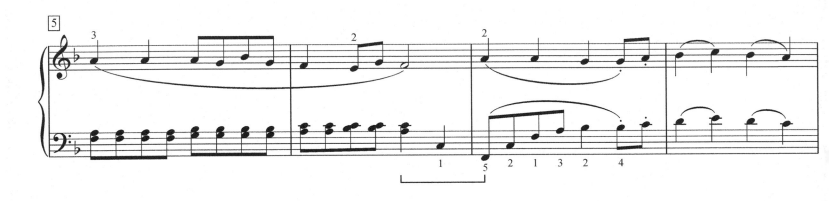

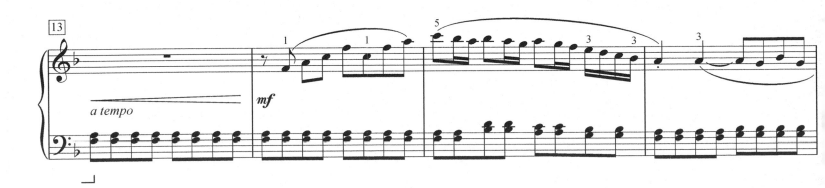

WERE YOU THERE?

Were You There

Traditional Spiritual
Arranged by Phillip Keveren

WHAT A FRIEND WE HAVE IN JESUS

Converse

Music by CHARLES C. CONVERSE
Arranged by Phillip Keveren

Floating, with rubato (♩ = c. 88)

SOFTLY AND TENDERLY

Thompson

Words and Music by
WILL L. THOMPSON
Arranged by Phillip Keveren

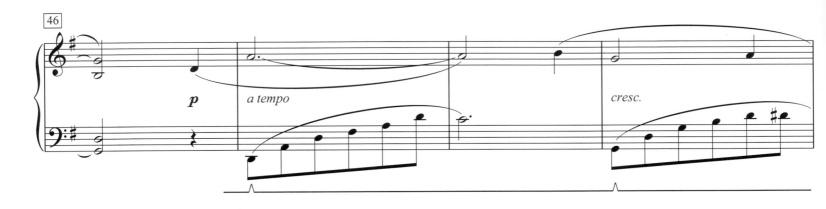